# China: 71 F
## Facts Fo ᴌus

*Malcolm Lee*

This book is just one of a series of "Fascinating Facts For Kids" books. For more fascinating facts about people, history, animals and more please visit:

**www.fascinatingfactsforkids.com**

# Contents

# Where is China?

**1.** China covers a vast area of eastern Asia. It is the fourth largest country in the world (after Russia, Canada and the United States) and is home to more than 1.3 billion people.

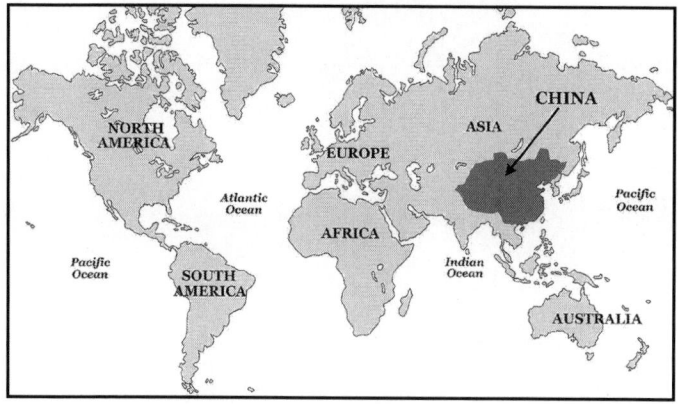

**2.** China shares its 12,500 mile (20,000 km) border with 14 other countries, including Russia to the north and India to the south.

**3.** China's 9,000 mile (14,500 km) coastline stretches from North Korea in the north to Vietnam in the south along the Yellow Sea, the East China Sea and the South China Sea.

# China's History

**4.** China is one of the oldest surviving civilizations in the world. People lived on the banks of the Yellow River in northern China at least 6,000 years ago.

**5.** One of the earliest rulers of the Yellow River valley was Huángdi, or the "Yellow Emperor", and he is regarded as the founder of Chinese civilization.

*Huángdi, the "Yellow Emperor"*

**6.** From around 2,000 BC until the early 20th century, China was ruled by a succession of powerful families, or "dynasties". A dynasty came to an end when rebels or foreign invaders overcame the ruling family and founded their own new dynasty.

**7.** There have been 13 ruling dynasties in China's history. The Zhou Dynasty (1122 BC - 256 BC) was the longest lasting, ruling for nearly 900 years.

**8.** During the Zhou Dynasty there lived a great thinker and philosopher called Confucius. His teachings of respect for family, school and country were a major influence on Chinese culture and are still valued in China today.

*Confucius*

**9.** Around 500 BC China was made up of seven different states which often fought each other to gain power. In 221 BC Qin Shi Huang, the ruler of the Qin Dynasty, conquered the warring states and brought them together under his rule. Qin Shi Huang had unified the country and he became China's first emperor.

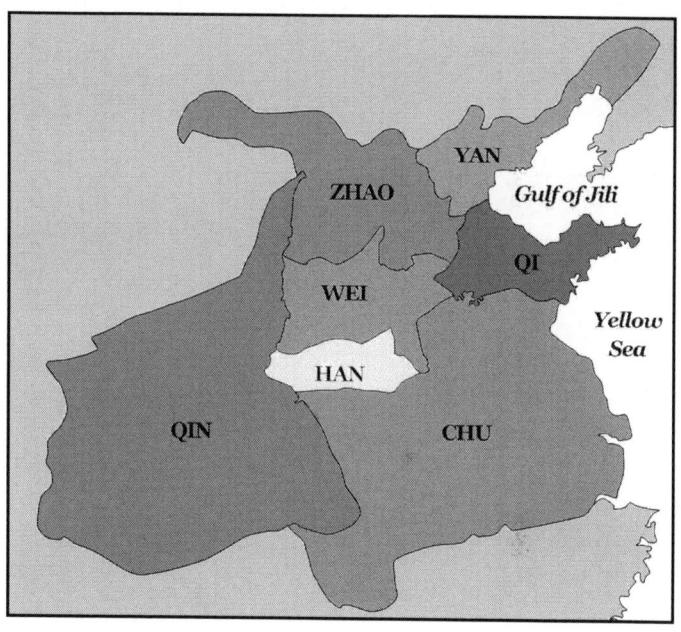

*The seven Warring States*

**10.** Qin Shi Huang was a ruthless and brutal ruler, but is remembered for great feats of engineering such as the building of a massive national network of roads and the construction of the 20-mile-long (34 km) Lingqu Canal, which is still in use today.

*The Lingqu Canal*

**11.**  Qin Shi Huang's most well-known achievement is the construction of a massive wall to keep out invaders from the north. Hundreds of thousands of convicts, slaves and peasants were used to build the wall, which eventually became the famous 13,000-mile-long (21,000 km) Great Wall of China.

*The Great Wall of China*

**12.** When Qin Shi Huang died in 210 BC he was buried in the then capital city of China, Xian. Sharing his tomb were thousands of life-sized model soldiers made of clay. The tomb was discovered in 1974 and the "Terracotta Army" has since become one of the world's most famous tourist attractions.

***Part of the Terracotta Army***

**13.** Following the death of Qin Shi Huang, the Han Dynasty took power and brought 400 years of relative peace to China. A sophisticated form of government was established based on the teachings of Confucius.

**14.** The Han Dynasty is considered to be a golden age in China's history and saw great advances in art, technology, politics and agriculture.

**15.** One of the major achievements of the Han Dynasty was the opening of the "Silk Road", a huge network of trade routes linking China with countries such as India, Persia, Arabia and Egypt. It even reached as far as Europe. The Silk Road brought great wealth to China and brought the Chinese into contact with other cultures.

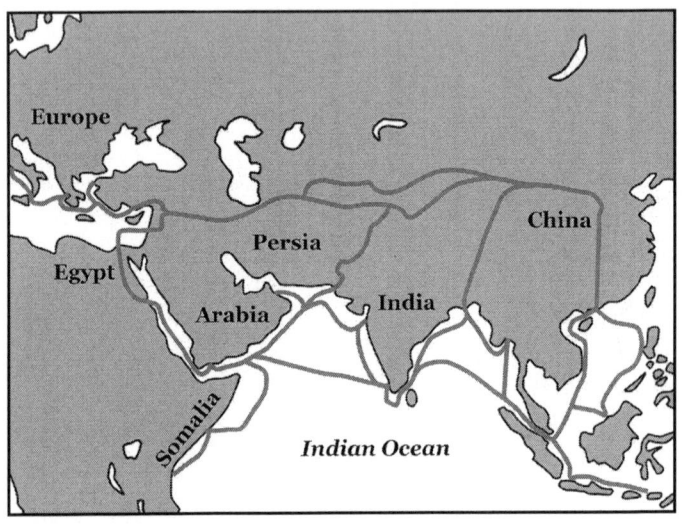

*The Silk Road trade routes*

**16.** In the 13th century China was conquered by the Mongols, who ruled over a great empire that covered much of Asia and parts of Eastern Europe. China became part of this empire as the Mongols founded the Yuan Dynasty.

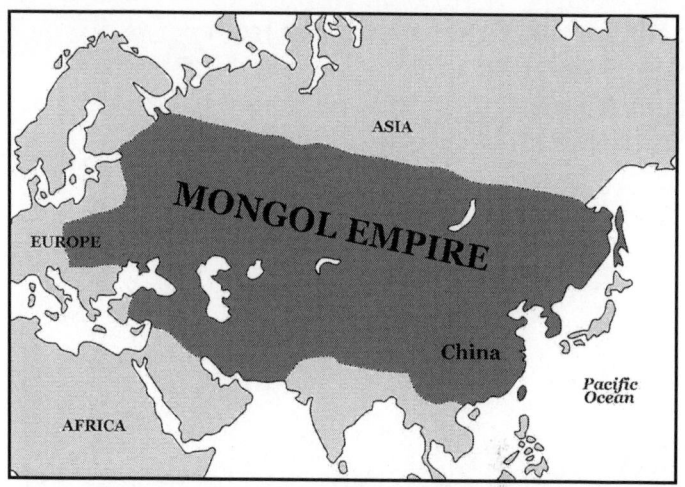

**17.** The Mongols ruled by force and were hated by the Chinese people. A series of rebellions finally ended in the overthrow of the Yuan Dynasty, which was succeeded in 1368 by the Ming Dynasty.

**18.** The Ming Dynasty united China again after nearly 100 years of Mongol occupation. The Mings ruled for nearly 300 years until another invasion brought about their downfall.

**19.** In 1644, another foreign power from the north, the Manchus, invaded and conquered China. The Manchus created the Qing Dynasty which ruled until the early 20th century and was the last of the great Chinese dynasties.

**20.** By the late 19th century, traders from many European countries were visiting China, although the Chinese leaders wanted to keep their country isolated and free from western influence. Many Chinese people thought that their rulers were wrong and demanded that China should be reformed and modernized.

***European traders on the Pearl River at Canton***

**21.** The Chinese rebelled against their Manchu rulers and overthrew the Qing Dynasty. In 1912 China was declared a republic, which allowed the Chinese people to have a greater say in how their country was governed.

**22.** Two political parties emerged from the new republic, the Nationalist Party and the Communist Party, each with different ideas of how the new China should be governed. The Nationalists wanted a more western and democratic system of government, whereas the Communists wanted the state to be in control of everything.

**23.** The Nationalists and Communists plunged China into a long and bloody civil war as they fought for control of the country. The war was the third biggest in history after World War One and World War Two.

**24.** After years of fighting, the Communists emerged victorious and took control of China. The Communist leader was Mao Zedong and on October 1 1949 he renamed the country "The People's Republic of China".

*Mao Zedong*

**25.** Mao's rule was brutal and hundreds of thousands of his opponents were murdered while the Communists were in power.

**26.** When Mao died in 1976, his successor, Deng Xiaoping, began to modernize China and bring more contact with the rest of the world.

***Deng Xiaoping***

**27.**  Today, although China is still a Communist country, it has adopted many western ideas and the country and its economy have been transformed. Chinese people today have more money and a better lifestyle than at any time in their history, although they still have little say in who governs them.

# Climate & Landscape

**28.**  Because of China's huge size, the climate and landscape vary greatly. There are high, snow-covered mountains; dry, sandy deserts and vast forests and swamps.

**29.**  The highest mountains are found in the south-west of China and they surround the huge Tibetan Plateau, which is the highest plateau in the world. It stands three miles above sea level and is known as "The Roof of the World".

**30.**  The highest mountain in the world is to be found on the border between China and Nepal. The peak of Mount Everest is 29,029 feet (8,848 m) above sea level.

*Mount Everest*

**31.** China has three great rivers, the "Yangtze", the "Yellow River" and the "Pearl River". The Yangtze is the third longest river in the world, flowing for 3,400 miles (5,470 km) before spilling into the East China Sea.

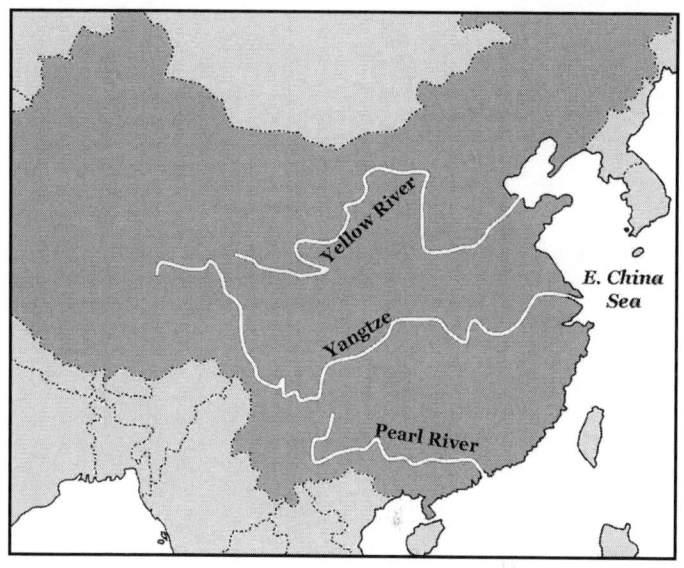

**32.** Because China is such a mountainous country, only a quarter of its land can be farmed. Farmers cut terraces into hillsides to provide more land area for growing their crops.

*Hillside terraces*

**33.** The best land and weather for farming is found in the central and eastern parts of China, where there are wide, fertile plains and rivers to supply water.

**34.** Northern China sees a big difference in temperature throughout the year. Icy winds blow in from the north during the winter, but in the summer temperatures can reach 100°F (40°C).

**35.** Much of southern China lies in the tropics and has lots of rain and warm weather all year round. During the summer the south-east coast can be hit by typhoons which bring strong winds and flooding.

# Life in China

**36.** More than half of the Chinese population lives and works in the countryside or villages. Farmers grow their own food and keep animals such as pigs, chickens and ducks. They make money by selling their produce in local markets or by selling it to the Chinese government.

**37.** Life in the countryside has changed little over the centuries. Sowing and harvesting are often done using hand tools and people work in the fields from dawn until dusk. Families live in simple houses made from clay or stone.

*A Chinese farmer*

**38.** Millions of Chinese live in cities which have grown massively in recent years. Many people moved from the countryside in search of jobs and a better lifestyle.

**39.** The largest city in China is Shanghai with a population of 22 million, nearly three times bigger than New York City's! Beijing, the capital of China, has a population of 19 million.

*Shanghai*

**40.** The economy of China has grown in recent years and the lives of millions of Chinese have improved because of this. Many Chinese have good jobs in the cities and live in modern apartments.

**41.** Many Chinese children go to kindergarten when they reach the age of three, before they start school at the age of six. They spend the next nine years attending school after which many will go to university.

**42.** The Chinese enjoy holidays and festivals throughout the year. The most important is Chinese New Year which lasts for two weeks and is a time of feasting and celebrating with family and friends.

**43.** Every June the Dragon Boat Festival takes place on rivers and harbors throughout China. For three days, huge and colorfully-painted dragon boats race against each other to the sound of beating drums. The boats are paddled by teams of up to 22 rowers and the prize for the winners is to have happiness and good luck for the coming year.

*Dragon boat racing in Hong Kong*

# Language

**44.** Chinese is the oldest language in the world, having been spoken and written for around 6,000 years.

**45.** There are many different versions of the Chinese language, but the main one is Mandarin Chinese which is spoken by more people than any other language in the world!

**46.** Unlike western languages which are written using an alphabet to form words, Chinese is written down using special characters, which are like little pictures. Each character has its own unique meaning.

*"Harmony"*　　　*"Light"*　　　*"Courage"*

***Chinese characters and their meanings***

**47.** There are around 50,000 characters in a Chinese dictionary, although you only need to know around 2 - 3,000 to be able to read a Chinese newspaper!

**48.** A Chinese word can have more than one meaning depending on how it is said. The word for "mother" can also mean "horse" if it is said in a different way!

# Art & Culture

**49.** China has a long history of producing beautiful art, including paintings, porcelain and music.

**50.** Chinese paintings are created on lengths of silk or rice paper which are mounted on scrolls to be rolled up or put on display. Inks and dyes are used rather than paint and popular subjects include landscapes, flowers, birds and people.

**51.** China is famous for its porcelain, having produced beautiful vases, pots and bowls for thousands of years. The world famous blue and white vases from the Ming Dynasty are bought and sold today for millions of dollars.

*A pair of Ming vases*

**52.** China has a long tradition of music making. Musicians play on bamboo flutes and string instruments which are plucked and bowed to create the distinctive and mysterious Chinese sound.

*Chinese musicians*

**53.** Chinese opera began during the Song Dynasty (960-1259). The Opera tells traditional stories using music, singing, dance, acrobatics, mime and even fencing!

**54.** Nowadays western classical music is incredibly popular in China. Millions of Chinese children learn to play western musical instruments and the major cities have their own orchestras and concert halls.

**55.** Chinese culture is full of ancient myths and legends, many of them telling tales of mythical animals such as the dragon, the tortoise, the phoenix and the qilin. All of these creatures are respected and revered as symbols of good fortune.

**56.** The qilin has horns on its head, scales on its body and the tail of an ox. It can roar like thunder, spit fire and has a life span of 2,000 years!

*A statue of a qilin*

**57.** The most important symbol for the Chinese people is the dragon. These mythical creatures have supernatural powers and are seen as symbols of strength, courage and goodness.

*A Chinese dragon*

# Food & Drink

**58.** Chinese cuisine is well-known throughout the world, with many western cities having their own "Chinatowns" devoted to Chinese restaurants.

***Chinatown in London, England***

**59.** With China being so immense, there are many different types of cooking found throughout the country. They include Cantonese from the south and Sichuan from central China.

**60.** Cantonese food is the cuisine most familiar to westerners. Fresh meat, fish and vegetables are stir fried, steamed or roasted, and seasoned with ginger and soy, producing rich and wonderful flavors.

**61.** Sichuan cooking uses chili paste or dried chilis to produce hot and spicy dishes. A well-known Sichuan dish is "Kung Po Chicken" which is stir-fried chicken, peanuts, vegetables and chili.

*Kung Po Chicken*

**62.** Stir-frying is a very healthy way of cooking. It uses very little oil and the high temperatures used means that most of the nutrients are retained in the food.

**63.** The Chinese use chopsticks to eat their food with. These are 10-inch-long (25 cm) lengths of wood or plastic, square at the top and rounded at the end which picks up the food.

## *Chopsticks*

**64.** Sharing meals is an important part of Chinese family life. Lots of different dishes are put on the table at the same time and everyone takes a small amount of each one to put into their bowls.

**65.** Tea is the traditional drink of China, having been an important part of Chinese culture for centuries. There are lots of different types of Chinese tea, including teas made from flowers such as chrysanthemum and jasmine.

# Assorted China Facts

**66.** The mountains of central China are home to giant pandas, the only place in the world where these animals are found. The clearing of the forests where they feed means that the panda is an endangered species, but steps are being taken to make sure it survives.

*A giant panda*

**67.** The last Chinese emperor, Pu Yi, was just six years old when he was overthrown in 1912. He became a gardener and died in 1967.

**68.** During the rule of Mao Zedong, he wrote his "Little Red Book". The book was full of quotations from his speeches and every Chinese person was expected to carry a copy of it at all times.

**69.** It is thought that China gets its name from the Qin dynasty. "Qin" is pronounced "Chin" in Chinese and could easily have evolved into the word, "China".

**70.** The Chinese have a rich history of scientific discovery, technology and inventions. Accomplishments in these areas include the invention of paper, gunpowder, the compass, silk production, porcelain making and the umbrella.

**71.** The flag of China was first flown in 1949 when the victorious communists created The People's Republic of China. The background color of red is the symbol of revolution, the large star represents the Communist party and the four smaller stars symbolize the Chinese people.

*The Chinese flag*

# Illustration Attributions

**Huángdi, the "Yellow Emperor"**
uncertain [Public domain]
{{PD-1923}}

**Confucius**
National Palace Museum [Public domain]
{{PD-1923}}

**The Lingqu Canal**
Farm [CC BY 3.0
(https://creativecommons.org/licenses/by/3.0)]

**European traders on the Pearl River at Canton**
William Daniell [Public domain]
{{PD-1923}}

**Mao Zedong**
??????????? (unknown) - http://sarbaharapath.com/wp-content/uploads/2015/11/Mao2.jpg, Public Domain,
https://commons.wikimedia.org/w/index.php?curid=538
79271

**Deng Xiaoping**
Author unknown [Public domain]

**Mount Everest**
Rdevany at the English Wikipedia [CC BY-SA 3.0
(https://creativecommons.org/licenses/by-sa/3.0)]

**Hillside terraces**
Raffaele Nicolussi [CC BY 3.0
(https://creativecommons.org/licenses/by/3.0)]

**A Chinese farmer**
Takeaway [CC BY-SA 3.0
(http://creativecommons.org/licenses/by-sa/3.0/)]

Printed in Poland
by Amazon Fulfillment
Poland Sp. z o.o., Wrocław

53789125R00022